Nobody Left Behind:
A Printed Words A₁

Raising money for

Mustard Tree

Edited by Amanda Nicholson

Word from the editor

After the first charity anthology (*Words to Remember*), I was pleased to donate the profits to Cancer Research and Marie Curie.

I hadn't planned on doing another because it was time-consuming and my own work had finally picked up. However, with the recent cost-of-living crisis, I had so much I wanted to write about and highlight. Instead of just rambling on, I thought it would be better to let other people speak out and publish their poems, prose and non-fiction to help amplify their voices. So, that's how this anthology came into existence.

As the editor of *Nobody Left Behind*, I thought it was important to only edit when it was absolutely necessary, to allow everyone to have their say in the exact way they want to say it. For this reason, some of the work included is in non-traditional formats because it was sent to us that way and/or the author specifically requested for it to be published that way.

Choosing my own pieces to include was probably more difficult than selecting work from the talented writers we accepted for this anthology. I had so much I wanted to say, but in the end, I knew I couldn't cover everything. The other voices in this anthology cover different aspects of the struggles many of us face, but it's impossible to include everything, and it's difficult for some people to be open about their experiences.

For every person who has shared their thoughts and experiences in this anthology, there are countless more who suffer in silence. I hope that the money raised through this anthology will help them in some small way, and the awareness will make anyone reading this think twice before passing judgment.

Nobody should ever be left behind, regardless of gender, race, ability, health, or anything else.

Togetherness
(Elaine Savage)

Walking in the rain, him with his umbrella as I wore my carrier bag from Lidl.

Romantic surprise of sharing a bag of chips, instead of being taken to a boring restaurant.

Despite living in the car, I am loving my new kitchen. A gift from the pound store, a blue washing up bowl. Who cares about running water when you can see the sky in a bit of plastic. So romantic every night. A view of the stars. I only need stick my head out of the car window. Who needs leg room to sleep, when you can get your leg over whenever you fancy, gearstick permitting.

We also have our very own bar. Yes, almost a pub. Whoever said that White Lightning cider was a few sups short of a cocktail, has little taste. Indeed, our clientele come from all walks of life. Some are steadier on their feet than others, but they all are connoisseurs of the nectar, which is also unkindly labelled, "loony juice". Indeed, we have come to call this park bench our own, after the car was repossessed.

Still, we keep the romance alive. On balmy nights I take off my wig, and we dance to the rhythm of the sirens, never forgetting our honeymoon, back when he was prime minister, and me his paramour.

If only.

Foxy
(Elaine Savage)

The local foxes have started to befriend me, probably because I smell, having cut down to one shower per week, to save on the leccie. The other night, I got out of my car and there was one of our local foxes, just looking at me.

The fox came over and sniffed me, nodded his head in an approving way, obviously not showering much is an advantage in fox land. I followed him, and soon we came to his lair.

Not a lot to write home about structurally, but inside it was full of foxes who were holding what looked like musical instruments. They were fashioned from bits of wood and had strings which looked suspiciously like they had come from living creatures, as they had flecks of what looked like blood sticking to them.

Having travelled around a bit, and observed that people have different customs, I try and fit in where I can. Imagine my surprise when one of the foxes offered me an instrument. It was not the guitar or banjo of my dreams, but it did have 4 strings. Nothing in the way of frets, but then my fretting was enough.

I began strumming the instrument and singing. Initially, the foxes seemed happy. Halfway into my set, one of them stood up and said, "We were promised Springsteen, if we made the instruments." Then they all started to get angry.

Well, I did what any red-blooded woman would do in those circumstances. I offered them a recording dcal.

And that is why me and the Feral Slow Foxes are trying to hit the big time.

Bio

Elaine writes poetry, comedy pieces and songs, which she performs as Riley Savage. She is the video manager for Semitone Studios, a music studio located in Marple. In 2015/16 she achieved a distinction from Access to Music in Manchester, where she did the artist development course. Elaine recently graduated from Bath Spa University, with a merit in her master's degree in song writing. To see/hear Riley's work, go to her website:

https://www.rileysavage.co.uk/

I'd Give My Vote
(Philip Burton)

In an ideal world I'd give my vote to
Clement Attlee
(Prime Minister from 1945 – 1955)

or someone not a shyster or a banker
someone who could stand and talk, but not AT me
and that was Clement Attlee

yes, I'd have gladly voted for Clement Attlee
accused of arriving at Number 10 "in an empty taxi"
implying he was a nothing, a nonentity

but he wasn't
he quietly got on with the job
yes, I'd have gladly voted for Clement Attlee

but – as there IS no Clement Attlee –
I'll aim to give my vote to someone newly poor
or someone misunderstood

one thing for sure
I'd give the world for Clement Attlee

Bio
In 2019, Philip Burton concurrently held four poetry competition First prizes, including the Jack Clemo, the Sandwich (Kent) Poet of the Year, and the Barn Owl Trust. Philip received a commendation from Heidi Williamson in The Poetry Society's Stanza competition, 2020, for his poem on the theme of dyslexia. In 2021, he won the East Riding Poetry competition. His publications include *The Raven's Diary* (Joe Publish 1998), *Couples* (Clitheroe Books Press

2008), *His Usual Theft* (Indigo Dreams Press 2017), *Gaia Warnings* (Palewell Press 2021), and *The Life Dyslexic* (Palewell Press 2022).

To Survive the Crisis
(Michael Burton)

All you've got to do is splurge a little less,
graft a little more, consolidate your debts.
Smoke roll-ups, drink ASDA brand rum,
cut out all things marked frivolous and fun.
Ditch your Netflix, your Prime, your iTunes.
Delay your nights out till early next June.
Reduce your gas and electric use,
your want to be warm is no good excuse.
Sell the books you bought and read them online,
the bus station in town now has free WIFI.
Replace with haste your taste for lattes,
from now on no breaks from black Nescafe.
It is all in fact just as simple as that -
the courage, the patience is all that you lack.
Learn from the man in the flat next to yours,
grateful for the scraps he can barely afford
or the mother you walk past almost every day,
offering herself for some overtime pay.
It's time for you now to follow their lead,
forget all your talk of the corporate class greed.
There's enough to get by if you just sacrifice
all that you have that comes with a price.
Life after all has its booms and its busts
just make do with less and don't make a fuss.

Crisis, What Crisis?
(Michael Burton)

There's peace on earth like never before,
enough jobs for us all on warehouse floors,
enough houses - or at least caravans -
there's stocks in the shops or that's the plan.

We've still got our schools and our not-so-crowded prisons,
the crime may be up but the violent type hasn't risen (much).
We've still got our phones and our oh-so-loved devices
and we've never known such low avocado prices
So.....crisis, what crisis?
Crisis? What crisis?

There's police in our streets and most we can trust,
there's so many shows online on Disney plus,
there's never been a time more people had degrees.
Soon we'll have more of them than we have trees.

We've mobile games and for singles - dating apps.
we're never lost now we've got Google Maps.
By all comparisons this is bliss,
life's never been close to as good as this!
Crisis, you ask? What crisis?
Crisis? What crisis?

There's solar panels and windmills all around,
no coal plants or gasworks to be found.
No teenage smokers anymore,
no immediate threat of civil war.

So what's with all this dull and dreary news?
Don't you know there's always other truths you can choose?

You might as well take this hit
cos it's never you or your lot who'll decide this.
Crisis or not, we say, what crisis?

Bio

Michael Burton is from East Lancashire in the UK and his poems have been published most recently in The Interpreter's House, The Honest Ulsterman, and Pennine Platform. He also writes and performs as NotAnotherPoet and is the vocalist in the band, New Age of Decay. Their debut album can be found on all major streaming platforms.

Blue Collar/White Collar
(Isabelle P Byrne)

Goat hoofed hands protrude from crisp cuffs.
White collar creased around a sweaty scruff.
Haven't we had it all, haven't we had enough?
No room for evil to give it to us rough.
We are the blue collars that discolour in the light.
We are the union of people that have been pushed out of sight.
No more will we listen to the devil to tell us our needs.
No more blue collars shall be sacrificed or brought to our knees.
Starve us out, turn off our lights, take away our tenacity, take away our rights.
You chose the wrong people to oppress and start a fight.
We are so learnt in being wronged; we know just how to get it right.
We are the ones that fight, the ones that shall bring the rest of us to the light.
So goodbye dirty white collars you've shown your worth.
You've shown to us all that there is no place for you on this earth.

Bio
Isabelle P Byrne is a published poet whose work focuses on identity, mental health, society, sexuality and nihilist thought. She has been interviewed and had her poetry broadcast on *BBC Upload*, *Hannah's Bookshelf* (North Manchester FM), *The Sunday Tea Show* (All FM) and *Spoken Label* (Andy N's podcast). Isabelle has also been interviewed by *Big Issue North*. Her book, *Pandora's Ruin*, can be purchased through Bent Key Publishing, or ordered through Waterstones. https://www.bentkeypublishing.co.uk/product-page/pandora-s-ruin-isabelle-p-byrne

The Solution
(Richard Harries)

The solution is not easy
Small things
Like growing food
Community orchards
Could help
Recycling
Repairing
Reusing
Not wasting, not throwing away

But radical change is needed
The two-party corrupt system
Has not worked
Has never worked
The Tories are vile
Self-interest and greed abounds
But Labour are leaning to the right
No Corbyn in power
And his attempt at a party
Has no MP standing yet
And his defeat by the sewer press
Campaign to vilify him is now years ago

We need control and transparency
On the earnings and interests of MPs
We need to have reason and logic
Common sense to rule politics
Revolution could bring this
But as it has in the past
Revolution can bring worse things
More vile corruption and power abuse

So we need major and radical reform
Of Parliament, of power
Banishing corruption
And the vast storage of wealth in tiny pockets
Reform!

Bio
Richard Harries is a Yorkshire poet. He has been writing and performing poetry and stories for over ten years, and performs all over the North of England. Richard's work covers many genres. He can be political and angry, write children's poems, comedy and so much more. His serious work includes poems about male breast cancer, homelessness, depression and disability discrimination. He is signed to Stairwell Books of York and has published two books; *Awakening* and *Iconic Tattoo*.
https://www.stairwellbooks.co.uk/product/iconic-tattoo/

Hard Times Call for Furious Dancing
(April Manderson)

Hard times call for furious dancing
So I'm making militant moves
Because a simple sway of the hips won't do
When we're all being had for fools
I've been trussed up for 44 days
And a wild winter waits for me
I'm fairly sure that the last time I checked
Body heat was still free
So hard times call for furious dancing
And I think that time is now
Gonna 'shake what mamma gave me'
For all I'm worth, and how
Gonna call upon my ancestors
Raise my head into the sky
Tilt my body backwards
Then feel the beat and fly
And move it, move it (one –time!)
Move it, move it Bruuuup!
Move it, move it, give it up and turn it loose
Like no-one's watching, when everyone's watching
And there's nothing left to lose ...
But this fucking government!!
Let's dance into the revolution
The best things in life are free
And hard times call for furious dancing
So come and dance with me

Bio
April Manderson is a counsellor, who works primarily in education settings. She
is a passionate advocate for holistic wellbeing approaches, a proud mum of a

fantastic young person, a research fellow at MMU School of Education, and a founding member of a community writing collective.

Untitled
(Martyn Hesford)

she
is one of the millions

paying their rent religiously
never falling behind
with their bills

scraping a life

together

they were taught in school
"God is good"

and now

in her last years
this old woman

left
on
a door step
like the milk bottles
once upon a time
used

she looks
into my eyes

saying nothing

her hands tremble
reaching into a plastic bag

she feeds the birds with breadcrumbs

doing good

only giving

I could see
hidden in her face
the little girl
she had
once
been

did she notice
this coming I wonder?

the bottom of the pile
the end of everybody's list

those who do not count
those who do as they were told

once young

now old

her life used up by them

thrown away by them.

the breadcrumbs
gone.

Bio
Martyn is the writer of two collections of poetry, *Lilac White*, and *Snow Star*. His first novel, *The Moon is Blue*, was published recently. Martyn is perhaps best-known for his biographical drama of artist L.S. Lowry, made for theatre, radio, and feature film, *Mrs Lowry and Son*, starring Vanessa Redgrave and Timothy Spall. Martyn was also nominated for a BAFTA Award for his drama, *Fantabulosa!* starring Michael Sheen.

Comparing the Current Government to Being in an Abusive Relationship
(Amanda Nicholson)

I left an abusive relationship around 10 years ago. My ex never hit me, but he made me hand over all my money, spoke to me like I was worthless and let everyone believe I was the one using him. Why am I writing about it here? Well, the way the current government treat people is a lot like that relationship.

If you think I'm exaggerating, then one of the many examples I can use is Universal Credit. People who claim this are often in work, but because they claim a benefit they are seen as worthless by the right-wing media. If I had £1 for every comment-baiting news story that talks about people on Universal Credit and the so-called benefits they get, I wouldn't need to publish this anthology. I would already have enough money to solve the cost-of-living crisis in the UK.

What these articles all have in common are the uneducated and sometimes vile comments they attract. There will be dozens of people who proudly announce that they work and don't see why people who don't work should get everything. It's a good way of being able to tell who is lucky enough to have a well-paid job where their wages don't need to be topped up. That's great for them, but criticising other people who are working (but for bad employers) is focussing on the wrong group of people.

Much like an abusive relationship, this shift to criticising low-paid workers reminds me of the way my ex would let all his friends and family think I was using him and not contributing financially, then would play on the low self-esteem I had to make me feel worthless and lucky to be in a relationship with him. One night he even came back from the pub and was so proud of himself for turning down some woman who apparently came on to him. It's like the bare minimum you should expect, not to be cheated on in a long-term relationship, but again, I was expected to be grateful for whatever scraps he threw my way.

The right group of people to focus on are the government. They hold the power to get employers to pay a real living wage and to get rid of zero-hour contracts.

This would let workers earn enough to live without benefits, but just like being in an abusive relationship, it makes them rely on this 'help' and keeps their confidence low.

People are expected to be grateful for being so low paid their wages need topping up. Now, with rising energy costs and food bills rising at a ridiculous rate, we're all supposed to be grateful for money off our electric bills. These energy companies have made extortionate profits, but continue to raise their prices. Then the government took the option of using taxpayers' money to deduct money from their bills, which are still hundreds of £'s more expensive than they need to be, rather than consider renationalising gas and electricity or taking other steps to bring down the energy costs. So yes, we are meant to be grateful to get a little of our own money back. This reminds me of my abusive relationship where my ex would spend a big chunk of the money I gave him at the pub, then bring home a bag of chips for me and act like he was being generous, even though it was just a small fraction of my own money.

Here's where the differences end though. I eventually saw the light and left my ex, moved on, found someone worthwhile and married a man who respects me. The problem with the government is, so many of their supporters keep voting for them. They prefer to blame other people for the way things are, because they are an easier target. It would be great if they saw the light and realised any other government would be better, but will they? I guess only time will tell. We can keep telling them, but just like in my abusive relationship, I had to see the truth for myself and learn an important lesson.

Only Today
(Amanda Nicholson)

If today was the last day
To speak your truth
Before it was suffocated in lies
And retrieving it felt like wading through quicksand
Would you finally speak freely
Or continue to say you don't do politics?

If today was the last day
To show how you feel
To forget about self-imposed barriers
And hear what others have to say
Would you continue to talk over them
And play the same broken record instead?

If today is all you get
To make a change
Will you still put off until tomorrow
With wafer thin excuses
Or will you take your last chance
Before everything you take for granted is stripped away
And you're left out in the cold forever?

Bio
Amanda Nicholson is the editor of this anthology. She has written several novels under the name "Amanda Steel", including *Ghost of Me,* which was shortlisted in the 2020 Author Elite Awards.
Amanda also works as a copywriter and article writer. Her published credits include Reader's Digest UK, Ask.com, Jericho Writers, Authors Publish and Introvert Dear.
Her blog is https://amandasteelwriter.wordpress.com/

Hell's Blog
(John G. Hall)

it's another damn day
of doings and sayings

of four walls, port holes
and lethal torpedoes

it's another damn day
of sleep-in, freak out

two eating for one
and poisoned TV

it's another damn day
of dancing on razors

of bleeding nonsense
and hearts amputation

it's another damn day
of lies about lying

of money bombastic
as life goes quietly

all out of sanity.

The Chills of Chance
(John G. Hall)

Her revolution starts
with this scratch card
and ends in the food bank

with a bag of white sugar
assorted canned products
and starvation weaponised

into a sponge soaked in
vinegar on the spearhead
of a savage absent class

head down she rubs harder
then blows the silver away
and begins to scratch again.

Bio
John G. Hall was founding editor of radical arts magazine, *Citizen32*, and was
a political activist in the 1980s. John was published in *Emergency Verse* and
The Robin Hood Book - edited by Alan Morrison. Also, in volumes 1,2 and 3
of *Best of Manchester Poets*. His collection, *Poems for Explosion*, is published by
Crisis Chronicles Press, Cleveland. His latest book, *Making the Dark Visible*,
is published by Some Roast Poets Publications. He runs the Manchester Beat
poetry night - Beatification. For the past 10 years, he has organised a writers
retreat on the Island of Arran, Scotland. He has a degree in English Literature &
Creative Writing from the University of Salford.

Life Hacks
(Laura Taylor)

I've heard you can run a car on
nothing but good faith, if you're careful.
Who's for soup? I make it out of stones,
fill our pockets with them afterwards.
They make you feel fatter, like your ribs don't rattle,
and the hunger doesn't matter
when you drown.

I read something somewhere
you can make your gas go further if you never
put the heating on or dress in
feather boas and an old string vest.
Who's for stew? I make it out of dew
and fresh air, feeds a family of four
for a year, maybe more, with a side
of despair and mashed depression.

I was advised that a cap is not a cap
in that way. Not protective, a cover, a lid
to keep the wayward in, to stop mad dogs
making profits on the back of destitution.
Who's for chips? I make them out of
little bits of fluff, fry them in a dream
I once had about grease.
They taste of greed and unremitting grind.

I've been told that you don't really need to keep clean;
just shower in the rain, let the trickle-down
bathe you in its piss.
Who's for cake? Eton Mess, layers of
distress and sell your pet

to pay the rent on
affordable homes.
Serve with loans and filthy lucre
for a weekday cheat.

Bio

Born into a working-class family in the north of England in 1968, Laura Taylor has challenged arbitrary forms of authority all her life. She believes in the power of poetry as a means by which silent voices speak and hidden ears listen. Now in her prime, she
understands fully the potency of kindness in a world intent on creating division. She has three collections published by Flapjack Press - *Kaleidoscope*, *Fault Lines* and *Speaking in Tongues* - and performs her poems at venues and festivals across the UK.
She can be found here: https://fb.me/LauraTaylorPoet
and here: https://www.writeoutloud.net/profiles/laurataylor

Everything in the Middle
(Andy N)

You understand poverty all too well when your father was told back in 1982, his job at GEC in Trafford Park was being moved to London. He led a walkout before then leaking the story to the press, refusing to spend a month down south teaching somebody else his job.

You understand poverty all too well when he then spent the next eighteen months out of work and struggled over two Christmases with three young children, not sure where his next penny was coming from as he became increasingly worried about how they were going to survive.

You understand poverty all too well, with worn-out shoes and outgrown pants and the relief on his face when he got a new job in 1984, only for his relief to change to stress overnight, surviving on less money, and he had to start doing overtime just to ensure he could pay all the bills on time.

You understand poverty all too well, nearly 40 years later, when after your pay was frozen for years, you were given notice that your job was going and told it was a call centre or nothing. You were left there repeating your father's actions, starting a new job with extra hours just to keep going.

You understand poverty all too well, whether in 1982 or 2022, and you see the similarities between the times with constantly rising bills, strike threats and the real fear of returning to that winter of 1978 when you had repeated strikes and no real end in sight to the misery.

You understand poverty all too well, with train workers going on strike and Royal Mail, whose managers are reportedly trying to force their staff onto a zero-hours contract, mirroring everything that went on before and a government who seem determined to bring the country to its knees.

You understand poverty over your lifetime and your father's and the pattern that crawls its way over our very existences, whipping our feet from underneath ourselves, making us realise things aren't that different from Victorian times. Repeating into the 21st century and everything in the middle.

Haikus
(Andy N)

Your heater remains
switched off the colder it gets;
an abandoned prayer

***

merging the margins
millions fall off the edge
not enough money

***

Outside a food bank
when once you would have helped out
you now need their help

Bio
Andy N is the author of several poetry books, the most recent being *From the Diabetic Ward: Volume 1*, and he creates ambient music under the name of *Ocean in a Bottle*. He co-hosts Chorlton's Spoken Word night, *Speak Easy* and runs /co-runs Podcasts such as *Spoken Label*, *Cloaked in the Shadows* and *Storytime with Andy and Amanda*.
His blog is: https://onewriterandhispc.blogspot.com/

December Air
(Jay Rose Ana)

Frozen moments of Winter.
Pause all warmth of hope.
Fractured memories splinter.
Another season, struggling to cope.

Heating or eating.
Despondent choice.
Waiting a week.
To hear another voice.

Two knocks at the door.
Panicked, I hide away.
I tremble under blanket.
Don't knock no more.
Not today, go away, go away.

"Are you alright in there," the letterbox speaks.
The decibels rise with more knocks at the door.
"Are you okay?" My imagination peaks.
The monster at the door, hear it roar.

"Let me be!" my voice betrays.
My tears speak the truth, my arms tightly fold.
"Go away," I say. Please stay.

"Just checking you're okay, it's getting kind of cold.
Please don't think me rude, I've bought you some food.
I didn't mean to give you a fright.
It isn't much, I'm afraid, it's all I could afford.
I'd love to give it to you in person and check that you're alright.
I'll pop by this time again tomorrow.

For now, I will leave it here, by the door."

I stare, shifting focus, as I dig deep in my chair
Piercing cold, and lonely, December air.

"You're not alone," the letterbox tells.
"My children made you this picture."
"They'd love to give it to you themselves."

"There is just us, too", I hear a sigh.
"And this year has been hard", a gentle cry.
"Harder than most, I'm afraid, and I would appreciate a chat."
"So, I'll pop by again tomorrow, if that's okay,"
"What do you think about that?"

Clinging onto a moment.
As it gently slips away.
Like a breath upon the air,
Evaporating, until I see it no more.
I cannot control my thoughts.
But right now, I try and hold on tight,
So it cannot get away,

"Yes," I whisper.
"Yes, please," to the door.

Bio
Jay Rose Ana is a Worcestershire poet, originally from the heart of the Black Country in the UK. She is the founder of Mini Poetry Press, host of Words Collide Poetry Open-Mic, and host of The Poetic Podcast, her work can be found at https://www.jayroseana.com/

It's Okay Not to Feel Okay
(Nigel Astell)

You okay?
Yeah sure
Issues hidden
Short term
Secured safe
Multiplying themselves
Mood swings
No longer
Able to
Stop onslaught
Complete breakdown
Mental instability
Human kindness
Comes calling
Asking again
You okay?
This time
Not really
Is the
Expected answer.

Permanent Black Hole Engulfing Us All
(Nigel Astell)

Solving one
Another prevails
Endurance tested
Frustration encountered
Stress instability
Overwhelming problems
Never-ending challenges
Perseverance responds
Solving one
Another prevails.

Bio
Nigel is a member of the Stockport Write Out Loud poetry group. He likes the valuable support of personal friendships, which bond strong positive energy to produce a higher level of enjoyment to his writing. He is known for his explicit poetry. However, he often produces more serious work, usually to the acclaim from the other group members of, "You wouldn't expect that from Nigel."
https://www.writeoutloud.net/profiles/nigelastell

False Promises
(Donna McCabe)

Spewing political propaganda
For votes of office
Actions and promises
Needed actions
Quickly spilling away
Into the drain

Rusting Remains
(Donna McCabe)

Washed up remnants
Of a once sophisticated society
Rusting and corroding now
Through sheer ignorance and depravity
Pieces of a much larger puzzle
Of how humanity messed up so badly

Bio
Donna McCabe is an established poet with over twenty years of experience. Her work has gained her multiple accolades within her field of literature. This includes being published in journals, magazines and anthologies. She is also a respected admin on social media pages as well as having her own Instagram Page: @donnamccabe_
Facebook: Poemsbydonnamccabe

Feels Like My Birthday
(Dorinda MacDowell)

National Assistance, my Grandma used to call it;
the toffs giving handouts to the likes of us.
Nothing's changed., except the name.
Same old platitudes, same old patronage, same old struggles.

I thank God for potatoes: so many ways to cook them and they're filling.

Good job my fella left, really, all his money went on booze.
Just me and Billy now, he's nine, and he's a good kid.

Well I can't wait to see his face when he comes home from school
and smells the shepherds pie cooking.
Got some tinned minced beef at the food bank,
chuck in some peas and spuds and a bit of gravy:
Bob's your uncle!
I'll tell him I had mine earlier; I don't think he notices when I'm lying.
I'm not that hungry anyway. Not really.

I'm happy today, though, landed a part-time job,
cleaning at the Swan.
Cash in hand, so sod the bloody Tories.
Never trust a man jack of 'em, my Grandma used to say.
By God she was right.

When I get paid, I'll treat me and Billy
to fish and chips from the corner shop.
He'll think it's his birthday
Feels like my birthday as well!

Up early tomorrow to be at the Swan for six:

what a Godsend that job was!

We'll be all right, me and Billy;
I'll make sure of that.

And to hell with the bloody government!

Bio

Dorinda MacDowell is a mother, grandmother, lover of words, and a lover of life. She has been published in Work Town anthologies; had poems printed on the King Lear web page; won a poetry competition in a local publication, and been included in the list of finalists in a national poetry competition. Two of Dorinda's greatest pleasures are reading and playing with words.

Prices Kept on Soaring
(Ray Douglas)

She'd always seemed to struggle
Yet somehow made ends meet
Clothed her loving daughter
Put shoes upon her feet
But as prices kept on soaring
Red letters brought the heat
Too much was upon her plate
But none of it to eat
Starved by consequences
Stark choices thick and fast
Her benefits so pitiful
She could barely make them last

They'd always watched their pennies
Always put their children first
Satisfied their hunger
Quenched their every thirst
But as prices kept on soaring
Their pennies weren't enough
Queuing at the foodbank
For proud parents, that was tough
Compromised by consequences
Their marriage showed the strain
The children caught between them
Feeling that they were to blame

She'd always felt triumphant
With the business she had grown
Built it up from nothing
Except the courage she had shown
But as prices kept on soaring

Her overheads were overdue
Closing down her pride and joy
Such a joyless thing to do
Bankrupt by consequences
Depression now; not pride
Not unlike her humble home
She felt empty, cold inside

She'd always been so prudent
Her age made her that way
Rationed by the purse strings
Saved for a rainy day
But as prices kept on soaring
The rainy days became a flood
Her nest egg; broken, shattered
Her good sense did no good
Frozen stiff by consequences
The stress, the strain, the strife
The soaring cost of living
Came to cost her very life

They'd always made a profit
Fat cats fuelled by greed
A bonus in the pipeline
More than they'd ever need
And as prices kept on soaring
They lined their pockets even more
Rubbed their hands together
Energised themselves for sure
Filthy rich by consequences
Their callousness displayed
The soaring cost of living?
That's the windfall they were paid

Bio

Ray Douglas is a children's author, poet and illustrator from the North West of England in the UK. He started publishing his work in 2018 and continues to create funny, illustrated poems and stories for the young and the young at heart alike. His books include - *The Silly Sausage Saga and Other Silly Rhymes*, *Lucy the Tooth Fairy's Last Chance and Some Pretty Witty Ditties*, and *Gold Medal Hunters*. Ray loves visiting schools and other locations to spread the joy of creating and sharing stories with children everywhere.

The Doctors Say I Have Nine Lives
(Linda Downs)

9. The ride home from work ended with black ice
Porcelain bones, wrapped around grey metal and blue enamel
Life and death fighting for power, amongst the wires and beeps of intensive care

8. I stare up from my hospital bed at the sterile ceiling, of the Sistine Chapel
And I am Michelangelo creating a fantasy world with pretend paint
While depression, the constant eraser is scratching away at the colour hope

7. At night the pain hammers along damaged nerve endings
The black dog growls in the shadows of my lungs
The sheer weight of his presence shrinking their capacity to scream

6. Stitched together I appear whole again
A network of agony dulled by pink and white pills
A fragile vase, a patchwork of glue, so easily shattered again

5. Unable to work, reduced to a diagnosis I still need to eat
So, as the government begging bowl demands
I jump through hoops till I am dizzy and confused

4. Initiated into the world of Universal Credit and disability payments
I become just an email; no emotion allowed unless it is gratitude
My issues must be logged in the online journal, so they can monitor my spiralling
descent

3. I am invisible, a Dickens character, poverty has reduced me to nothing
The view from this poor house has remained unchanged for over a century
The black ice is back this time on the inside of the windows, and I am sliding

2. Oncoming headlights blurring my vision

My Journal pleas go unanswered, my phone out of credit
My anxiety says this is only what I deserve, that I am worthless

1. Winter rubs its hands in glee, sucks the warmth from this early grave
My mind lays back in the great depression, I have nothing left to bank on
Still, all is not lost, I have a stash of pink and white pills, a skeleton key to oblivion

0.

Bio
Linda Downs works as an advocate with people who have mental health and addiction issues. She has featured in various anthologies and has been writing for several years. Linda has recently started performing her work across Manchester.

Public Relations
(Lucy Power)

'We don't think you can make the poor parts richer by making the rich parts poorer'
Boris Johnson's Levelling Up speech, July 2021

With dreadful smiles the politicians say
we understand how difficult it seems.
We're well aware the future's looking grey,

with one in five in poverty today,
so we'll economise and modify our schemes.
With dreadful smiles the politicians say

we'll have far fewer banquets, less soufflé,
and streamline all of our investment teams.
We're well aware the future's looking grey,

but we cannot sell the flat in Saint-Tropez,
or lose the party's richest funding streams.
With dreadful smiles the politicians say

that the mistress needs the Porsche, so that must stay;
and the golf, the boat, and the mansion with oak beams.
We're well aware the future's looking grey,

so here's some food bank beans, and a doorway
for your cold hard cardboard bed with duck-tape seams.
With dreadful smiles the politicians say
we're well aware your future's looking grey.

Bio

Lucy Power is a poet, musician and artist living in Manchester. She originally trained as a fine artist, but her multiple sclerosis began to limit her practice, so she looked for other ways
to create art. Lucy has a Master's in Creative Writing. Her writing involves contemporary situations and diverse characters, and aims to make the hidden visible, elevate the everyday, and highlight the overlooked. Her poems are published in the Flapjack Press collections, *The People's Republic of Mancunia* and *NeurodiVERSE*, and the Commonword anthology, *Indivisible*.

Decus Et Tutamen
(Steven Wailing)

All my life in the presence of pound coins
won't be time enough to decode the words
etched on their sides but they mean
business to my creditors I've heard

the clinking colloquy of coins in hand
it says "Look after the pennies we'll
look after ourselves" What they don't say
they'll leave only pennies to pay the bills

Bastards Things won't add up but are good
at subtraction Money swears it says
"Fuck off out of here" "Pleidol Wyf Im Gwlad"
which is to say "Give me all you've got

and I'll still run out the door Bye!"
and off it trots to someone else's till
But then more coins come along say "Hi,
we've got Nemo Me Impune Lacessit pal

we'll buy you the earth heaven hell
a whole warehouse of consumer goods
that will never be yours Now sir please
sign on the dotted line each fortnight

we'll barely keep you alive a fickle
bunch eager to be spent bartered
exchanged for thin slices of action"
There goes another old friend off to

squander itself When it's all gone
I'll count out the change from zero

lose it in my pocket full of holes

Bio

Steven Waling's latest publication is *Lockdown Latitudes* (Leafe Press). He lives in South Manchester, and works two jobs, neither of which provide enough money to live off in this age. He performs his poetry wherever he is asked.

Exposure
(Rosemary Moore)

Politicians spend money
Investigating parties, they're dying
From exposure of their flaws

You: overspend on fuel in November
get overdrawn in December
By January it's frigid but
your overdraft is rigid
Come February, snowdrops peek
through snow,
in bed, your toes are warm
Cheeks red, nose drips
In the kitchen
cupboards bare
Shiver
Cold
Reactions
slow
Enzymes
Slow
No return
Hypothermia

Bio
Rosemary Moore is an active member of Ribble Valley Stanza and Clitheroe
Writing groups, and enjoys performing at open mic events locally. She also hosts
an international online creative writing group called Creatives Connected.
Rosemary has published a collection of poems called *Walking the Ribble Way:
from Sea to Source: poems for your journey* (2021)
She has other poems published, most recently: in *This Place, This Poetry Map
- Lancaster Lit* Fest (2022) and *Saving Face in Masks* Anthology 7 (Worktown

Words 2021). Most of her writing is inspired by nature and travel. She teaches Biology and Environmental Science, and has lived in China.

Letter Full of Love
(Eve Nortley)

My darling Fran,
I am writing to tell you how much I love you - as I know I don't tell you anything like often enough.

We are facing tough times, as a nation and as inhabitants of planet earth and I'm hoping that you will wear the love I'm sending you like a suit of armour, to protect you against pettiness, injustice and the self-serving super-rich who seem determined to wage war on mankind.

On a more mundane, but still important note, I wanted to talk to you about soup! Always a warm and heartening subject - apart from Vichyssoise, which, in my opinion, is a very unpleasant French swear word.

In straightened times when purses are empty and stomachs hungry, soup is a cracking culinary choice - especially if you can "sling in" red lentils or butter beans to boost the protein and iron quotients.

My top tip is to make your soup in a pan with a tight-fitting lid, bring it to the boil for 2-3 minutes, then turn off the fuel and leave it to cook in the residual heat for 10 minutes. Try your veg and if still not cooked, repeat the process. It's a bit more labour-intensive than the traditional "simmer for 45 minutes approach, but uses a lot less fuel. You may need to add a little more seasoning than usual, but it's still cheaper and just as nourishing.

If you can find a couple of soup-loving friends, organise a social soup swap where you each make 6 portions of soup and swap 2 portions with each friend, which will give you all enough soup for a week and 3 flavours for the cost of one. You could even be wildly adventurous and share a meal and some laughter... Always the best medicine!

Hopefully, your soup swap will save you enough money over a month or two to get your hair or nails done. Looking good has been a woman's battle dress for centuries - just look at Boudica. I realise woad may be out of fashion, but I'm sure Rimmel or Estee Lauder will have a modern equivalent.

Having covered Love, Food and Beauty, I'm going to finish this letter as I'm exhausted.

Sending you sunshine, love and laughter so you can shine a light in the darkness,

Mum

Bio
Eve Nortley is a Birmingham-born writer with a passion for ecology, heavy rock and Birds Custard. She has a background in the NHS and academia. As a performance poet, she has shared her work countrywide, on festival stages, to the central reservation of Preston New Road, in support of the environment, and the right to peaceful protest. Eve is the co-author of 2 collections, *Love and Lust in Bury and Rochdale*, and *Driftwood,* with Christopher Bainbridge. She has recently published a collection of poetry and prose, paying homage to her own "town", *Born to Brum*. She is currently performing as half of the innovative comedy duo: Chalk & Cheeze.

Breaking News
(Gordon Zola)

Well, Paddington's five minutes of fame, didn't last long, did it? Suella Braverman's only had him arrested and shipped back to Peru as an illegal immigrant.

Snow White's had to claim Universal Credit, since they closed down the mine and made the Seven Dwarfs redundant – and if you think Grumpy was bad before, he's less than happy at having to 'Sign On'.

Tin Man's still waiting for a heart transplant, on the NHS...been over a year now. Scarecrow got his brain, though. Went private, didn't he? Turns out he was in BUPA.

The Three Pigs are still trying to keep the wolf from the door...Alice, isn't in wonderland anymore...and Tom, Tom, the piper's son, is doing a two-year stretch, in Strangeways. I wouldn't mind. It was his first offence, and the pig wasn't even big enough to feed his family.

Humpty Dumpty is a shell of the egg he used to be. And Georgie Porgie's on remand for date rape...The less said about that, the better.

Baa Baa Black sheep is suing the council, for racial discrimination – and Old King Cole got busted for possession. There's strings attached. He should get off with it. Which is more than can be said for the Knave of Hearts. He got caught red handed with the tarts, again. Comes from a broken home, you know – can't kick that jam habit.

Sadly, the Owl and the Pussy Cat, two refugees who set to sea in a beautiful pea green boat, were arrested at Dover, and are awaiting deportation to Rowanda.

The Old Woman who lived in a shoe, remember her? The single parent with all those children. Well, she hasn't got that problem anymore? The kids got taken into care, and her home got repossessed. She couldn't keep up the payments on a state pension, could she? You'll find her slumped in Sainsbury's doorway every night.

There's one success story though. Little Miss Muffet. The vertically challenged, nervous girl; scared stiff of spiders, had counselling, didn't she, and became one of the country's top influencers. She formed 'Arachnids Are Us'...and streamed a weekly keep fit, webcast: 'From Tuffet to 5k in 5 Weeks', from her company's website.

Unfortunately, she lost everything when Bill Gates, took over the Web...and her fear of spiders returned. Last I heard, she was eking out a living on Babe Station as a Web Cam Artist.

All these titbits are fantasy. A figment of my imagination. They bear no resemblance to reality...or do they?

Bio
Gordon Zola (Edam good) has performed and hosted comedy and poetry, the length and breadth of Great Britain - and beyond, for over 25 years. He's released, (though some say it escaped), a musically backed CD: *No Strings Attached*, a poetry collection: *The Wheelie Bin Years*, (which some people say wasn't rubbish) and 2 CDs with anarchic band, Bard Company, in addition to being published in numerous magazines and Anthologies. He's currently performing as one half of the innovative comedy duo, Chalk & Cheeze - and writing a Novella: *Enlightenment is a Cup of Herbal Tea*.
Website: www.gordonzola.me.uk[1]

---

1. http://www.gordonzola.me.uk

Resources
(Carol Laidlaw)

This week, I more or less told my electricity company to piss off. For a few years, they had been sending me wildly over-estimated bills while refusing to accept my meter readings. They finally sent out their own meter reader, agreed my figures were correct, and we got the bill straight. Then, a couple of months later, they sent me a letter saying that they were going to double my electricity charges. I wrote back and told them I was going to pay them £100 per month, because that is as much as I can afford and if my bill turns out to be more, they will have to wait for the rest until my income increases.

However, my consumption this winter will be low because I do not intend to use the heating. They had the cheek to write back to say that doing without heating is "inadvisable" and gave me a list of debt management charities to approach. I used to have a paid job as a debt adviser and I know everything there is to know about managing money. I sent them back something of a rant, asking how they imagined half the country is going to be able to afford heating this winter thanks to their greed?

I'll accept that they have to make up for increased costs, but I resent that they're making huge profits on top of that. It so happens that doing without heating for most of the winter is nothing new to me. My original job was in the voluntary sector and depended on public funding. Since the Tories spent a decade cutting public funding, there is no money available now to fund my kind of work and they effectively killed my career. Since 2016, I have had only a few short-term jobs with long periods of unemployment in between. That has forced me to be very economical and very resourceful.

Of my household bills, rent comes first, always, water comes last. Water companies cannot cut off a person's water supply simply because they are too poor to pay. For three years I didn't pay them at all. When they applied for a county court judgement, I applied for a grant from the water company's trust fund. United Utilities has its own fund, which it can use to pay people's water arrears. Once they have given you a grant they expect you to make sure you don't get into arrears again. That's not workable if your water charges are still unaffordable. But I worked out a solution to that. It came from something I read in The Guardian, one of their voyeuristic articles about how poor people manage. It seems that the largest part of a household's water consumption is what comes out of their toilet tank. But you don't need to use the whole tank for every flush. Nor do you need to use clean water. I set up a water butt in the small yard I have acccss to and started collecting rain. There's plenty of rain in Manchester! I should mention that my water is metered. Now every day I dip a bucket in the water butt and use free water to flush the toilet. I use the washing-up water too, effectively using it twice. I have halved my water consumption and my bill. United Utilities is happy and I have one less source of financial stress.

I never compromise on food. I said rent comes first. Food comes second. I have never gone short of food and I make sure I never will. Making sure I have enough, and enough variety gives me a sense of stability in a precarious life. But I would never use a food bank. Having to beg a charity for something as fundamental as enough food to eat? It's too demeaning for me. And too frightening.

Almost any job would improve my situation, if I could only get one that lasts more than a few months or weeks. The one useful feature of Universal Credit is that it allows single people, not just families, to get the equivalent of tax credits. Even if I take a part-time job, I'm unlikely to be worse off. Getting the job is the problem. Employers seem reluctant to take on anyone over fifty and the feedback I get from job interviews is that they only want to hire people who have done the exact same job before. I have enough transferable skills to be able to do several jobs, besides my original calling, so I get job interviews regularly. What I don't get is job offers. I need to retrain for something new. The job centre is of no use in that respect, its only function is to police people's benefit claims. This month I have registered with a local charity that gets funded, among other things, to help older people work. They say they have to get a third of the people they take on into sustainable work. Let's see if they can come up with something.

What I can't do is mark time until I can get my old age pension because that's eight years off yet. Within that time, I would like to earn enough again so that I'm not constantly walking a financial tightrope. Whether the cost-of-living crisis will eventually tip me off the tightrope, or perhaps I should say, how long it will take, I don't know. I've only just cleared my debts this year after my latest short-term job, which lasted until May. I expect I'll have to start paying for food and fuel on the credit card again. But I intend to hold out as long as possible before I do that.

Bio
Born in 1964, Carol Laidlaw is a native of Liverpool and was a welfare benefits and housing adviser for 21 years. She now lives near the South Pennines and spends her time writing fiction and non-fiction and being politically active.

Gilbert *
(Scott Fellows)

The night lays down dark, deep
as the faithful in their graves.
He sits with his years in a room
filled with utility furniture,
fashioned, like him, during
an old war.

His single bar electric fire
grows faint and dies amongst draughts
that barge through cracked windows,
warped doors, the damp that seeps
through sponge walls
into skin and bone.

Each night, remembering grows harder
as faces grow faceless.
Faithless, he sings a tuneless waltz
he once danced with her
until, gripped by cold,
he stiffens into
an endless sleep.

* Some years ago, I lived next door to an old chap named Gilbert. He lived alone after the death of his wife with very few visitors, his two sons never visited. I managed to get him some home care as he was housebound, but only once every three days. He had a very limited income, just his state pension, which really wasn't enough. As often as I could, I would do a bit of shopping for him or sit with him, but I had a young family at the time and didn't have time to do more. After a few months, the council made some cuts which meant the home care stopped. I moved away and went abroad to work soon after and lost touch with Gilbert. Years later, a friend told me that he had been found dead in his house.

The cause of death was hypothermia. There had been a particularly cold snap that year and when he was found, it was discovered that he had nothing left on his prepayment card for the electric and therefore for heating. He had frozen to death. I hate to think how many people are in a similar position now....young or old. I wrote this poem in his memory.

Bio

Scott Fellows is an author and poet. He retired in 2014 from a career in education, as a teacher, both in the UK and abroad, headteacher and finally OFSTED inspector. In recent years, he has worked as a chaplain and counsellor in colleges. He has three books currently in print and is preparing a new poetry collection to be published later in 2023. He completed an MA in Creative Writing in 2015 at Manchester Metropolitan University. Scott lives in Stockport with his wife Pam and Suki, a dog with attitude.

Pensioner's Lament
(Roz Ottery)

Winter, blanket of cold, mantle of dark,
Pushes forward; hardening poverty's desperate heart.
No matter how we try to end this hardship we are waking.
Those in power don't know the impact they are making

Breath, laborious breath, steady, soft and slow.
Fending half-truths, with anger: Where I refuse to go
Hidden fears wear down my smile... despite the giving.
Meanwhile, our pensions shrink each day we're living

Mind, phlegmatic mind, of the rich and in control.
It's a circus we cling to, but the "familiar" pays a toll
We watch the homeless huddle, in a life they cannot alter
and there's the dread we all will follow if we falter.

Life: Laborious life. It's simply shifting grains of sand:
Ebbs away now, slipping through our reliable, upturned hands.
You see, we saved for 'a rainy day'... in preparation...
now we watch it disappear into inflation.

Oh, those mesmerising screens Unhurried flat and 'cool'.
Teaching our kids their worth lies in designer clothes at school
And the struggle's on, resisting all this nonsense.
All I seek is authenticity and conscience.

Bio
Roz Ottery started Britain's first singing telegram business in 1979. She wrote thousands of personalised songs for special occasions all over London; for ordinary folk and for the Rich and famous. Roz won the *Daily Telegraph* 'New Business Of The Year' award in 1981. As a performer, Roz enjoyed 6 years of success on the professional stage, in drama and musicals. She was in *Summer*

Rep with Gareth Hunt, Brian Murphy and Pat Phoenix (all stars in their day) and played 'Magenta' in the National Tour of *The Rocky Horror Show*. She has recently adopted her great-grandson and is now Kinship Carer to him in her retirement. This has caused joy but also financial hardship, hence her contribution to this anthology. The poem reflects the new struggle and challenges in the UK during 2022.

Willing Prey
(Mark Heathcote)

Given glass ceilings
we're all ring-fenced
drown in rank, tall-growing reeds
that'll sedge up all our sweet inlets
While they widen their bitter, greedy outlets
they bask like piranhas, ready to leap and feed
they'll snap at anything that breathes.

So we must hover
like wispy blue dragonflies
and drink in stillness the morning dew
we must, on balance, be their willing prey
tremble and fall like autumn leaves
and yet resist combusting into living flames
somehow we must soar, soar without wings.

Bare on the emptiness, their stewardship brings
and live with barely enough money or hope.
Given glass ceilings
we're all ring-fenced
we're all metaphorically milked
it's an unwritten agreement
they own us.

Bio
Mark Andrew Heathcote is an adult learning difficulties support worker. He has poems published in journals, magazines, and anthologies, both online and in print. He resides in the UK, and is from Manchester. Mark is the author of *In Perpetuity* and *Back on Earth*, published by Creative Talents Unleashed.

On the Phone to the DSS
(Marcel Maverone)

In order to direct your call,
we need to verify your identity.
It may be necessary for us to ask for
some of this information more than once
to enable us to put you through
to the same set of staff members
sitting in the same open-plan office -
please don't be put off by this.

Please provide the following information by
speaking slowly and clearly into the receiver -

What is your national insurance number?

What was the exact alignment of the planets
at the time of your birth?

How much of a soul have you retained thus far?
Round to the nearest decimal place.

On a scale of one to ten, with one being
common house fly, and ten being parasite,
how worthless to society is your current existence?

If you're ringing about a Universal Credit Claim,
please hang up and use the internet so we can
keep our employment levels at the absolute minimum.

If you're ringing about a benefit payment
that is not due yet, please wait until we've not

paid you before calling this number.

In order to direct your call, please listen to
the following options carefully -

If you are pre-existing, good for nothing
dole scum, please press one.

If you would like to reduce your benefit
entitlement by reporting a change of
circumstances, please press two.

If you're dead, please press three.

If you would like to be further deprecated
by a real live person, please stay on the line.

We're sorry, all our employees are busy
having a real job at the moment.
Please hold your breath until
an advisor becomes available.

Bio

Marcel aka Midnight is an underclass, queer, transmasc spoken word artist,
former community activist, and gobby little shit. He's performed at many
festivals, events, protests and political rallies, and award-winning shows, as well
as facilitating, directing and hosting several creative workshops and live
performances. An advocate of grassroots organising and the DIY ethos, his
performances have been described as a 'transcendent experience'. Primarily a
storyteller, with a healthy dose of gallows humour, he makes the personal
political, and the political relevant. Unafraid of grit and resistant to shame, he
has been known, on occasion, to summon storms.

No Vaccine for This
(Ruth O'Reilly)

I'm wearing a jumper
I'm wearing a hat
So desperate for heat
I'm hugging a cat
No I'm not sitting
Outside in the park
I'm here at my flat
Sat in pitch dark
Nothing is dropping
Except for my jaw
Cost of my shopping
Thrice the price of before
And we've all had our jabs
To protect from a virus
Yet we're dying instead
From an economic crisis

Bio
Ruth O'Reilly is a community radio presenter/producer with Allfm 96.9, who enjoys creating conversations with authors, musicians & poets from Manchester and beyond. She especially loves getting creative people through their first live radio interview & helping them to beat their impostor syndrome.

How It Looks from Here
(Rich Davenport)

Cronies and cover-ups
Tell us, "Shut up, submit to your betters"
In your eyes, there are no friends, no family
Just leeches and debtors

Smokescreens and loopholes
Spit on the truth and the law
The lives of the people below have no value
The bottom line is always "more"

Tell us, what's your motive, is it cold contempt?
Doing far too little, far too late
Cancer patients and war vets pay the price
Tip the wink to the old boys and hand out clean slates

Prey on the vulnerable, tighten the screws
The good Samaritan was slumming
You make no distinction between lazy and disabled
Just act like we all had it coming

While we're working longer for less reward
You try to steal the right to protest
While schools and surgeries are taking a hit
Those who strip-mined the economy hike up the interest

Shameless, blatant disregard
For the other 99%
A blind eye to the suffering
A deaf ear to the voice of dissent

We're sick of your lies and your racist scapegoats
Sick of your choking hands at democracy's throat
Sick of laws not enforced as you back-slap and gloat
You've sold this country down the river, while we're struggling to stay afloat

No more corporate welfare, tax breaks for the rich
We need equality and electoral reform
The poison we see at the top's the exception
The compassion we share at the sharp end's the norm

Bio

Rich Davenport is a comedy poet, stand-up comedian and musician from exotic Bolton, in the UK. Inspired by Spike Milligan, Ogden Nash, Billy Connolly, John Cooper-Clarke, Robin Williams, Benjamin Zephaniah, Victoria Wood, Lenny Henry, and by his friend and fellow Boltonian, the late Hovis Presley, Rich has gigged all over the UK, spreading mirth and making loud noises. No, he's never heard of him either. Rich was described in one review as a "no-nonsense Northerner," which is ridiculous, because nonsense is his business, and business is good.

Park Bench Paradise
(Mel Wardle Woodend)

Park bench paradise,
Sleeping outside.
Reddened, painful fingers fumble with thin sleeping bag zip,
You've nowhere to hide.

No door to close.

Outside you survive on adrenaline,
Nowhere is really safe.
Keeping your wits about you,
Hunker down, close your eyes, feel your heart race.

Some nights below freezing
Your heart barely beats at all,
It slows, almost giving up –
Mind and body succumb to the cold.

Hypothermia, pneumonia,
Frostbite, a transgression:
No job, no money, no money, no deposit, no deposit, no home –
You're stuck in this endlessly oppressive recession.

A mismatched shanty town

Of brightly coloured tents,

This isn't the third-world poverty of India, Nairobi or Mexico City...

It's 'affluent' England's Milton Keynes, seaside town of Falmouth and Tunbridge
Wells in Kent.

Thin fabric buffeted and blown; your shivering figure sits and waits
Cross-legged in the icy, biting wind
While a few feet away, rosy-faced shoppers burst busily into a cafe
To buy their customary coffee and cake within.

A row of brightly coloured tents

Lines a cold, grey, concrete underpass.
Their colourful cheeriness belies
Your bleak and empty eyes inside.

No door to close.

Mercury plummets into minus figures,
Yet you're all still stuck out here – the old, the young, the weak, the strong, the frail;
No one is exempt
From the risk of being derailed

From this rollercoaster ride of life - one minute you're sitting safely at the top –
Where you've found life's luxuries: A home, a family, a job.
Then – just one slip, one bad turn of the dice, you can fall and lose it all.
Kicked out, jobless, homeless; on the streets like a stray, downtrodden dog.

So, who is helping
To counteract your plight?
Who is helping you
Find a bed for the night?

A rise in unaffordable housing and benefit sanctions,
Work contracts for zero hours.
Employment is almost impossible

With no address – you are frozen – you've lost all power.

Soup kitchen volunteers
Dole out food and steaming hot tea;

Bringing cheer and warmth,

Sharing their own time generously.

But... your fight is getting harder;
Because people like you, who sleep on the streets
Are the ones we can see –
We know you've got no home, no bed, no warmth and not enough to eat.

But what about the hidden homeless?
Sofa surfers; relying on their mates for help....

Or night after night sleeping in a car

Just to get a tiny bit of shelter?

If you're really lucky you might land yourself a job!
Then your benefits will stop! Because surely you won't need them when you're
earning a 'living wage?'
Then, the old struggle resumes....
You've got money to eat but not enough to get a deposit to get off the streets and
into your own place.

You are working –
But for what? For who?
Lines drawn tight on your taut face;
The stress, the desperation of your situation starts to show through.

And slowly your resolve dissolves
As your life
Falls down
Around you.

So, what will you do?
How can you live your life?
With no door to close
In this park bench paradise?

Bio

Mel Wardle Woodend is a PhD student studying poetry and wellbeing through Applied Linguistics at Aston University and was Staffordshire Poet Laureate 2019-2022. Mel holds an MA in Creative Writing, enjoys facilitating poetry workshops and is co-organiser of WORD Stafford and Aston Society of Poetry. She is the director of dyslexia friendly publishing company Dream Well Writing Ltd: reflecting her passion for making reading and books accessible and enjoyable to as many people as possible. Her published poetry collections include *Natural Colours* (2017), *Just a Thought* (2019), a short story in *Tabitha* (2021) and various poetry anthologies for charity.

www.melwoodendwriting.com[2]
www.dreamwellwriting.simplesite.com[3]

---

2. http://www.melwoodendwriting.com

3. http://www.dreamwellwriting.simplesite.com

The Foodbank
(Ade Couper)

Foodbank.
The very word
Should strike fear
Into our hearts.
What sort of a world
Are we living in
Where it's accepted
That over a million people
Living in one of
The world's richest countries
Have to rely on charities
To feed them and their families?
Politicians and their press friends
Will glibly mealy mouth them
As "scroungers"-
Scroungers? Most of these people
Have worked harder than any MP
Or their friendly flunkies.
The pathetic bleating
Of publicity-seeking parliamentarians
Glibly and smugly spouting
"You can feed a family of four
On forty pence a day-
These people just don't know how to cook"-
As insulting as it is inaccurate.
If you can, as you say,
Feed a whole family
On forty pence a day,
Let's see you do it!
Time to put up or shut up
How about

Rather than vilifying
The folks who need foodbanks
We stop believing the lies
The politicians and the press keep feeding us,
And do something to help instead?
Let's give them a hand,
Let's show them we care-
Just pop an extra tin of beans in the basket
When you're doing your next shop
And pass it to the foodbank
For someone who needs it:
Someone just like you- or me....

Bio

Ade Couper is the former Worcestershire Poet Laureate (2021-22), and also works as a link worker for people experiencing mental ill-health. On a daily basis, he sees the effects that poverty has on the people he works with.

Quills of Inky Space
(Rhianna Levi)

Whether we prepare or not,
We all have quills of ink in our lotus blood lineage.
Pacing the floors to abide by all rational laws,
Yet protection for those in need is proclaimed an outrageous use of speech by
those high in roof pier towers.

Unfortunes of power are its corruptive misuse,
Which by classism and apparent rightfulness is perused.
This affliction of vocabulary is for all those who scream to find a listening ear in
times of bleakness.

To those who work because they desperately want to live,
But are drowning from biting bills that cut off their circulation not just at their
feet.

And this is for those who fight injustice with justice in arts of imperishable
goodwill.
Fondness whose advancement is further than global seas and corn fields.

Be sure to take up your inky quills,
Take up all the space you need—
Make sure that hymns, art, tears, joy, is never unspent;
Transform stung serpents into flour with aid of others,
Evade shamefulness in requesting pillars of encouragement and affection.

Like each pigmented quill compelled,
We are principally made.
Deter from accepting disruption from egotism branded by selected others.
Boldly write and denote for all your lungs, eyes, lips and heart unfathomably
desire.
Transcribe quiddity aloud beyond speaker phones.

Where Is the Kindness?
(Rhianna Levi)

Consequences are to be had,
When dear critical workers of our laboured society cannot touch heated food,
Even with their freezing hands within their homes,
Tallying shredding hair follicles in frenzied stress,
Adding to the depression infection.

No alternative routes permitted,
No security admitted,
A living crisis is not just that of economy,
But that of glass shards,
Scraping away emotional contentment.

Laid to the winter waste side in fright,
Set alight by the sludge on damp poor flooring.
Making sure people can live comfortably should never become boring,
At least not in spirits of the good-hearted.

Bio
Rhianna Levi is a teacher, academic, and writer. She is the youngest ever Worcestershire Poet Laureate, in tenure for 2022/23. Her writing and social media presence focus on social issues, spirituality, and humanity in the world.
Facebook: Rhianna Elizabeth Levi
Twitter: @RhiannaEliza98
Instagram: @RhiannaLevi98

Exit

(Phillip Carter)

Set in a near-future dystopia where Canada's 'Medical Assistance In Dying' scheme crawls its way to the UK and somehow gets worse.

we're a brave new world
with a new world order
where nobody is illegal
and no country has a border

and everyone is equal, and life is sublime
and if it isn't, we'll give you a deadline
and if you're too sick, we've got a little prick
because why live feeble when you can take the needle?
and if your condition stops you from seeing your friend
you can visit us for a shortcut to the end
and if you've got a mental illness
that keeps you out of work
we can ferry you into an inescapable chillness
beyond that final hypnagogic jerk

it's the modern equivalent of cutting the brakes on your wheelchair
and going for a nice long walk by the coast
and we know it's hard, no it's really not fair
to be solid when you could be a ghost

it's a final solution for the weary worker
a horror story to be turned into a tear-jerker
they'll tell it good in Hollywood when you're not yet cold
they'll write some pithy dialogue about how you never got old
they'll make it with that actor you despise

and he'll do your signature 'dead-face' and stare out with vacant eyes
and later get fired for biting the director's thighs
in the year twenty-five twenty-five

"In the year twenty-five twenty-five, when the poor are no longer alive
when we helped all the disabled die, you will cry
in year 2595, only the richest fucks will survive
only the wretched zombies will thrive in their hive"

and back down here it's a match m.a.i.d in heaven
and that's where you're going, with all the symptoms you're showing
you see, there's not much we can do,
(outside of upping your disability pay or helping you find purpose
but let's be honest mate, to society, you're not much more than surplus)

you're depressed, badly dressed
and perpetually in a state of itching unrest
but we'll make it civil, you can take the drug at home
if you'd rather die alone, or you could come to the clinic
don't be a cynic
you can't criticise what you've not tried
and guess what, you can't sue us once you've died
here at the home for medical assistance in suicide

yes, at the clinic we'll help you slip into something more comfortable
like the icy embrace of death
we'll make each moment tweetable, as you draw your final breath
and as you shudder toward oblivion
with each hypnagogic jerk
we'll turn and say to your friends
"Such a shame he couldn't find work"

because really, what's the point?
of being poor, disabled and depressed

when you could get it all off your chest
by having a government-assisted cardiac arrest

and when you're gone you can meet god
who I won't capitalise because I hate the sod
and maybe he hates us too and hates poems that end
prematurely because the author signed up to the...

**If you were affected by the message in this poem, please remember.
There's no harm in trying for Medical Assistance In Dying.**

Bio
Phillip Carter is an award-winning comedy poet and author of dark Science
Fiction. His debut book, *Who Built the Humans?* has been called 'genius' and
'blasphemous', once on the same day, and his talk show, *The Phillip Carter Show*,
picks up clever people and shakes them until funny things fall out. His books,
show, and free stories can be found at
https://realphillipcarter.substack.com/

Government Advice on How to Survive the Winter in Difficult Times
(Clive Oseman)

In times like these, you have to think outside the box.
Great nations are built on innovation.

Ride a bike to work to save on travel costs.
If you can't afford a bike
and it's too far to walk, ride a horse.
A horse may be hard to find on a housing estate
but no one said life would be easy
and it's not something many would try to find
so if there's one going spare
the effort will be rewarding.
In more rural areas a cow would be easy to find
and would do the same job.

Do not watch television.
That way, when the electricity supply is disconnected
you will already be used to the boredom.
Routine is good.
Do not see the world you're missing out on
through the tainted lens of the television camera.
It only fuels false hope.

Foodbanks are there for a reason. Use them.
It is important to eat.
You cannot reasonably be expected
to work to optimum capacity
if you are hungry.
Trickle-down only works if the poor do.

At the next election
vote Conservative.

Gordon Brown got us into this mess
and we inherited a bankrupt nation.
Next time will be different.
Honest guv.

When you feel down
take a look at the nice blue passport
you will never be able to afford to use.
Doesn't the look of it, the feel of it
give you a warm glow inside?
Isn't it great to take back control?

Keep warm by exercising vigorously.
Do not have sex. This can result in children.
People like you don't deserve children.
If you are disabled or have chronic illness
and cannot exercise vigorously
we'll declare you fit for work
and the stress will kill you.
Cremation is a good way of keeping warm.

Remember. We're all in this together.
We are all making sacrifices.
We love you all.
Together we can make this country
the envy of the world again,
a nation of equal opportunities
for all its native people.

God save the king.

Bio
Clive Oseman is a Swindon-based Brummie spoken word artist, comedian,
satirist and promoter. He is a multi slam winner, has performed at festivals,

headlined or featured at events around the UK and in New York City and performed at the 2022 New York City Poetry Festival. His third collection, *It could be Verse*, was published by Black Eyes Publishing in 2020. He is currently performing his one-man comedy spoken word show, *What if They Laugh at Me?* anywhere that will tolerate him.

Afterword

This anthology was created to raise awareness of peoples collective and individual struggles due to poverty, caused or aggravated by the cost-of-living crisis. Please share your copy or buy another for anyone you know who might benefit from reading this collection.

All the profits will be donated to Mustard Tree. They are a Manchester-based charity who do great work to help those in need.

Please check out their website and find out how you can support them.

https://mustardtree.org.uk/[1]

---

1. https://mustardtree.org.uk/

Lightning Source UK Ltd.
Milton Keynes UK
UKHW010641270123
416064UK00001B/86

9 798215 677896